PRAYER IN THE NEW AGE

Some further books of White Eagle's teaching:

PRAYER IN THE
NEW AGE

PRAYERS AND INVOCATIONS OF
WHITE EAGLE

THE WHITE EAGLE PUBLISHING TRUST
LISS · HAMPSHIRE · ENGLAND
MCMLXXX

*A much expanded and revised version of the
edition of 1957, itself a revision of
'Prayers of the New Age' (1942) and
'A Little Book of Prayers' (1937)*

*First published in this edition,
September 1978
Reprinted October 1980*

© COPYRIGHT, THE WHITE EAGLE PUBLISHING TRUST,
1957, 1978

ISBN 0 85487 041 5

Set in 11 on 12 pt Bembo

Printed in Great Britain by
FLETCHER AND SON LTD, NORWICH

CONTENTS

INTRODUCTION

'Jesus once said, I will show you how to pray. He said, when you go into your secret chamber, close the door. In other words, shut out the noise and turmoil of the outer world from your mind as well as your surroundings. Enter with humility and simplicity into the inner chamber of your heart and pray: "Our Father which art in heaven, hallowed be thy name. Thy kingdom come on earth." Now, where is heaven? What is heaven? Heaven is a state of harmony, heaven is a state of happiness. You cannot be truly happy amid all the noise and turmoil of the material world; therefore, withdraw from it into your inner self; go into heaven with your Father, and thus hallow the name of God. Then pray and work in your own life for God's kingdom to come on earth.'

These are White Eagle's words, about the beginning of prayer and meditation. White Eagle always works in the spirit of these remarks; he never talks as if man's contact with God only took place in some remote region, or as if such contact was limited to people of a very religious disposition. Many people, perhaps caught up in family life, or involved in public responsibility, have an intuitive contact with the worlds within and live close to an awareness of the spirit within them. And the spirit is within every man, that spark or seed of divine love. White Eagle has always endeavoured to help all those to whom he has talked, of whatever walk of life or habit of mind, to realise the place of their contact with God within their own heart. Listening to him it has seemed that he was revealing things that were always there but had been hidden from one's view. And this awareness of God within and around is found not by any straining —more by relaxing—but in the silence and stillness of one's own heart. One of the prayers in the first chapter speaks of seeking 'the place of purity, truth and love, within the centre of our being. We seek the Christ within, and through this inner Christ light we learn to worship thee our Creator, our Father Mother God.' It is through dwelling on and expressing the light of love within the heart that the soul comes to approach and to know God. The place of stillness within one's own heart is always there, rather as the spiritual path, the path of love, has been called 'the unsuspected path in your very midst'; but often it takes experience of happiness and sorrow, trial and error before the soul learns to recognise and seek the God within. Yet there comes the time in the life of every soul when a man consciously or unconsciously seeks the light of God to help him continue his journey, and to enable him to help his fellow men.

It is to assist his brothers in seeking the light of God that our elder brother, White Eagle, has given the prayers that make up this book; and to help them in their turn give their own service to human life. We hope that his loving words will help those who read them to come to realise and unfold the Christ spirit within their own hearts; and that they will be able to draw on them for inspiration, strength and vision as they, in brotherhood with the rest of life, seek to become a little more at one with the Father Mother God.

Although there are included in the book passages of White Eagle's teaching as well as the prayers themselves, the prayers and the teaching are without dogma or creed, and we hope will be a source of happiness for people of many differing outlooks—although united in their respect and love of the Christ spirit. Some people fear that prayer and meditation mean a turning away from life, as in the past perhaps they have. But they are really (among other things) a means of making sure that action and the soul's outer expression are inspired by the inner spirit and not by emotional or mental confusion, and of giving to life more genuinely. White Eagle says:

'You do not, on earth, understand the meaning of love. There is a great deal of talk about love but we would guide you to find love not in the noise and turmoil of the outer world, but in the depths of your own inner being; and if you can find that power within your own heart it will be expressed in your speech and actions and life spontaneously. You will not think about it, but you will express love in kindness and gentleness, sympathy, helpfulness. You will not preach, you will just "do" and in doing the will of your Father Mother God you will become a power, a radiant light which will touch other lives. The light will go from you, not necessarily through thought or in over-talking, but in the beauty of the spirit of God which you are developing within you.'

*

The origin and use of the prayers

Nearly all the prayers were in fact originally given in the context of a group meeting or service, and thus they all speak of 'we'. Although they have been left unchanged, they are easily adaptable and equally suitable for use on one's own, and many people may like to substitute 'I' for 'we'. In this way, the prayers in the first chapter of the book which were originally given at the opening or close of a meeting can be beautifully used as the beginning or conclusion of a personal meditation. Some users of this book may also wish to substitute 'you' and 'your' for 'thee' and 'thy' when talking of God, and should of course do so if they wish. We have left the language that White Eagle chose to use as it does seem part of his way of expression. The word 'amen', not printed each time in the book, can be a seal of strength.

A few of the prayers were spoken or written

by Grace Cooke or Ivan Cooke (the founders of the White Eagle Lodge), but they came naturally out of the inspiration of White Eagle's teaching and of working with him, and we have not separated them.

AT THE OPENING AND CLOSING
OF MEETINGS

In this chapter, each page carries an Invocation and a Benediction. White Eagle has always begun and ended meetings with prayers such as these. He seems able to communicate something of his own quietness of mind to others; and as he speaks in the stillness he is able gently but firmly to turn the thoughts of those present towards aspiration, and towards the light of love within; at the same time invoking the blessing of God, the Great White Spirit. He has always seemed to be assisting everyone to rise in consciousness, and bringing the love of heaven down to earth.

The benedictions and short prayers of thankfulness set a seal on the experience gained during the service, helping each person to hold onto the intuitions that may have come, as they take up—and take up with renewed happiness—the responsibilities of life again.

Entering a chapel or a lodge can be symbolic of turning within to the inner sanctuary; and these same prayers, occasionally with very small adaptation, can be used on one's own as an entry into meditation, as well as to help a group draw together in common aspiration.

We turn from the outer to the inner world, and in the silence and the stillness we seek deep within our souls the presence of our Creator, the source of life, Father Mother God. We seek the glory of the Christ within, opening our hearts to the incoming of this heavenly light . . .

In the quietness of our worship may our inner vision open to the reality and the glory of the world of spirit which is all about us; and to the companionship of loved ones in spirit.

As we make this contact, the light is stimulated in ourselves, and goes from us to bless all the world . . .

*

May thy peace and serenity bless us and the light of thy countenance shine upon our pathway henceforth and forever.

In the silence may we feel the holy presence of God, our Creator.

We open our hearts to the incoming of the light of God, praying that we may feel the impress of God's love drawing us all together in one spirit—those who are in the physical body, and the hosts in the world unseen.

We pray that we may realise this at-one-ment of spirit, and that during this service thy love may rise within our hearts and go out to all mankind, to all creation.

O gracious Spirit, we thank thee in humility for the expanding consciousness of thy goodness, thy love, in our hearts; and we thank thee for the knowledge of thy love and thy power to permeate our lives and lift them to thy world of beauty.

Let us be still within. We withdraw from the outer world to the inner sanctuary of the spirit, and there wait for the revelation of the light.

As we kneel before the altar within our souls, we are conscious of the light burning upon the altar. We worship the Source of our creation ... We worship the light of the Christos, the Cosmic Christ ...

We thank thee O Great White Spirit, Father and Mother God, for the blessing of thy love which we can now feel enfolding us, for the strength and power which arises within us, and for every opportunity this earthly life offers us to grow in spirit nearer to thy glory.

*

Good shepherd, may I sing thy praise within thy house forever ... The human personality is thy house O God. May I manifest thy love and blessing in my life and work forever.

We seek the place of purity, truth and love within the centre of our being. We seek the Christ within, and through this inner Christ light we learn to worship thee our Creator, our Father Mother God. We pray that we may draw closer to understanding thee, thy love, thy wisdom and thy power. May our inner vision unfold to reveal the life of the spirit in all its glory.

We remember before thee the need of all mankind, and pray that there may go forth from this service a beautiful light and healing power to bring peace to men's hearts, and to give spiritual healing to all who suffer in mind and body. We thank thee for every blessing.

*

We kneel before the altar in thanksgiving for the joy which fills our hearts and makes life perfect and good.

Infinite, all-pervading Love, thou who art the beauty, the light and the wisdom of life, we pray that all thy children here assembled may be responsive to the rays of love; that each heart may be open as a flower to the sunlight; and that in the expansion of love within, they may contact the realms of truth and power. Give unto their waiting hearts, the gift of understanding.

Great White Spirit of the open spaces, the mountain tops and the quiet peaceful valleys; Great White Spirit of nature and of the heavens above the earth, and of the waters beneath. Great White Spirit of eternity, infinity, we are enfolded within thy great heart. We rest our heart upon thy heart. Great Father and Mother God, we love, we worship thee; we resign all into thy loving keeping, knowing that thou art love, and all moves forward into the light.

We are still in thought, in body and in spirit; and in the quietness of our soul we meet the great shining Light, the source of all life, the great Father Mother God. Silently from our heart we thank thee, we praise thee, we worship thee; we surrender ourselves to thy will; and in the glorious presence of this shining light we find peace. We feel the power of this love, this protection.

For the blessing of the love which we now feel in our hearts, we give thanks.

*

O gracious Spirit, we have met together in simplicity and with love. We thank thee for the spiritual blessing which has entered our hearts. We pray that we may ever remember thy loving guidance and the peace which thy truth ever brings to the human heart.

May thy peace, thy truth, rest and abide in our hearts always.

In humility we enter the innermost sanctuary to invoke the blessing of the Most High, the source of life. May we be purified in heart and mind, simple and humble in our approach to truth. We pray at this moment that we may behold the shining ones, our silent companions from spiritual realms. May our understanding be quickened as our vision unfolds. May the blessing of the Lord Christ fall gently upon each waiting heart.

*

Let us raise our hearts to the great eternal Light. Our Father God, we thank thee for the joy of learning, for the light which flows from thee; we pray, O God, that we may walk in simplicity and humility gathering thy knowledge from the simple experiences of life. So may we live ever more in harmony with thy divine principles and find peace, the peace of eternity.

Almighty, heavenly Father, we meet together in unity of spirit, in brotherly love,
aspiring to the spiritual realms of wisdom.
May we all learn something of thy beautiful
truth, and carry forth into the world of action
the will and the power to express in human
life the beauty of that which we shall find in
communion with the spirit. Let us relax all
tenseness, brethren; be at peace and commune
within your breast with the Most High.

*

O God, Father of all living creatures: the
light of the mind and the love in the heart,
who doth sustain life in all its perplexities, who
doth control the elements, who art the perfect
life ... We pray that we may draw nearer in
understanding to the truth of our being. We
call upon the angels of peace to bring us their
stillness and the quietude of the loving heart.

We raise our hearts to the almighty Spirit, to all Wisdom, Love and Power, giving thanks for our creation and all the beauties of life, for the gifts of the senses, the gifts of the mind and the gifts of the spirit. We pray that every heart in this assembly may be touched with love and sweetness, and that the angels of the Christ circle may be able to draw close to this little group and give to it the beauty of their love.

*

With stilled minds and open hearts, we stand in silence upon the hilltop, with starlit skies above us, and hear the murmur of God's voice in the whispering trees ... A deep hush comes, and we know that God has blessed us. To him we give thanks for the love which brings this beauty to our hearts, and offer ourselves in loving service, praising him and his laws of life now and for evermore.

May we be united in love, recognising that our neighbour, whatever his path of approach to God may be, in common with ourselves, desires to find God and to serve his brother man. In this fellowship we include not only the human, but the humbler brethren of earth, of the animal and nature kingdoms—all living things. And we raise our hearts to the shining company in the world of spirit, recognising the service which they render to humanity.

We wait in the stillness of the spirit within, at peace with all life, to receive the spiritual outpouring from the centres of love, wisdom and power. We resign ourselves to the light of the Christ love and power ... In the stillness and silence of eternity, may we know the meaning of love.

*

May the Holy Spirit bless our work, and bring the joyous heart ... May the eternal peace of the great silence be with us now and for evermore.

We close the doors of our senses, and seek the silence of the spirit.

We aspire in spirit and in truth to the Great Architect of the Universe, our creator, the eternal spirit, the light and truth of all mankind. We surrender our personalities to the sweet influence and blessing of the eternal spirit and the beauty of higher worlds; to the love and the justice of God. We pray that during this service we may be lifted into a higher consciousness, into a true awareness of the spiritual life. And through the simple sincere love of our hearts may there go forth from this service a light and healing power which will bless and comfort and illumine many souls.

May the peace of the spheres of light be in our hearts. May the consciousness of the Christ spirit bless and beautify our lives now and always.

Let us lay aside all thought of the material world and seek to make contact with the Source of life. O gracious Spirit, all-enfolding love, light and life, we come before thee in humility and tranquillity of heart and mind. May nothing in us prevent us from stepping forward into the light; and when sorrow and trouble come may we willingly surrender to thy love and wisdom; knowing that underneath are thine everlasting arms: for thou art merciful and just and all-loving. May our hearts be open and minds subdued, waiting to receive the beauty of thy light.

O Father Mother God, we thank thee for thy infinite love. May these thy children go their way in peace, filled with thy holy spirit. Bless them, bless them, O Son.

Most high and perfect spirit, Great Architect of the Universe, we come before thee praying that thou wilt guide us in all our ways. May the wisdom of thy mind inspire our work; may the beauty of thy form be made manifest in our work; and may thy love inspire our every thought and action towards our fellow men. May we pass through life's journey with courage and humility as our companions and come at last into thy glorious presence—perfected through the Son, the Cosmic Christ.

*

To the eternal God ... silently, in our hearts, let us give thanks! And may our praise be expressed in joyous living, and caring with quietness of mind for the needs of every soul we encounter, the needs not necessarily of the body, but of the soul.

Great Spirit of Power, Wisdom and Love, great parent from whom we derive life, we pray that thy blessing may find response in us. May the lower self be set aside, so that we may respond to the light and the truth of thy spirit within our breast. Then we shall know thy great love, and our eyes will behold the beauty of thy handiwork . . . yes, even in that which appears to be unenlightened, may we see the beauty of thy work. For all these gifts of God, beloved Father Mother of our spirit, we thank thee.

*

Let us worship. Father Mother, giver of all the glorious gifts of life, we breathe in the cool, sweet air; and we receive the blessing of silence . . . we breathe in the breath of life, the perfect benediction of God. We thank thee . . . all is well.

Gathered in this upper room, we await the outpouring of the power and the love and the wisdom of God. We forget the physical body and the divers claims of life on the earth. We look up to the source of all life, our Creator.

We worship thee as Father—Divine Will; and Mother—the Wisdom; the Son—the Cosmic Christ, the supreme light, and the presence, the physical manifestation of light. Holy and blessed Trinity of life with whom mortals dwell, we pray to come into closer relationship with thee. We pray for the growing realisation of thy presence. We pray that every soul here in this upper room may be given a clearer, truer vision of the life beyond the limitations of flesh. We pray, O Lord, that these children of earth may be granted a vision of the great concourse on the heavenly planes, of those who are the true companions of the spirit while they journey through the darkness of matter. Dear Lord, may the sweetness of thy love be scattered like incense upon these dear children that they may seek communion, spirit with spirit, and be lifted out of the turmoil and inharmony of the lower life. May the presence of the Cosmic Christ Spirit bless and sanctify this gathering, and this work.

White Eagle's blessing

God bless you my brethren. God bless you, every one, in your search for happiness and truth, and in your search to give service to the world and help your brethren on earth to a happier state of life. Good night.

Let us pray in spirit to the source of our life, our Creator Father-Mother and the Son, the Cosmic Christ. We open our hearts in praise and thanksgiving for creation, for all the blessings of life, for the glory and the happiness which comes to us.

We thank thee O God, for the light of the sun and the gentle rain, the fruits and flowers of the earth and the bread of life, which sustains both the physical and spiritual needs of man. For all thy bounty and thy blessings, O Lord we thank thee. We pray that we may learn how to use thy gifts wisely and well, so that in the end we may come to thee full of grace, bringing a rich harvest of physical experience and spiritual life.

O God, we pray that thy ministering angels and the company of heaven may smile upon this little service that we may feel the blessing of the Most High, and the love and the truth in spiritual communion.

*

We turn our faces to the Great White Spirit and receive into our souls his love, his wisdom, and his power. We bless and thank him. May we become ever more worthy to walk in his light.

Beloved brethren, forget the physical plane. Try to become very still and calm within so that you may be attuned to the spiritual life. Around you are many from the spirit realms, some of them your own friends and companions of former lives. Beyond them are angelic beings; and the teachers, the saints and the perfected souls of all ages—all those who have passed through great tribulation in the world and have reached harmony with the divine law of life.

So, my brethren, with love in our hearts, we pray to our Creator, the source of all life, that the veil may be drawn aside between the darkness of the physical and the beauty of these higher realms of life, so that we may hold sweet communion with this shining host. We give thanks to thee O God, Father Mother and glorious Son, thy perfected one whom we worship under many names but who is the Christos, the Cosmic Christ. May the blessing of his love be with every one present now and always. So mote it be!

*

There are those here, invisible to some, visible to a few, bright souls who have come out of great tribulation, with garments washed whiter than snow. They bring their own light, their love; for they once walked the self-same path you follow; they knew suffering and grief. They bring the light which radiates from every sacred centre of the spirit. They pour upon you the light and life streams of cosmic energy, of healing for body and soul.

Even thus may the peace of the spirit, of the eternal life, bless and strengthen and lead you onward . . . may the harmony of heaven heal. Peace be with you, brethren, and the love of the eternal spirit shine through and enfold you.

We remember that holy birth, the birth on earth of the great initiate Jesus, through whom the Christ light shone, and ever shines onto the earth, and through the human heart. In the silence of the spirit our vision opens to the company of shining ones and angels who gather to adore the birth of the Lord Christ, a symbol of the birth of the Christ Child in the human heart.

May our ears be touched that we may hear the song of the angels. May we be sensitive to the enfoldment of their wings and learn to remember their touch of peace in our lives. Father Mother God, may the veil fall from our eyes in this hour of communion and worship in company with all creation; and may we glimpse into heaven and see love, your Child, your Son. In the silence and stillness of eternity may we know the meaning of love. O gracious Spirit our beloved Lord, we thank you for the Christ Mass.

'Where Jesus knelt to share with thee the silence of eternity, interpreted by love' . . . we think of this vision of the Master Jesus, with light radiating through him, the light of peace and the light of love, bringing healing to all who come within his aura. Let us open our souls to his inspiration, and understand the ideals of true living, of service towards each other, and of the growth of God within. We pray that we may be true, worthy channels in his path of service. O God, may light and healing go forth from us to comfort the sad and the suffering, and give courage to those who must fight the good fight. May we who worship here go forth recharged and rededicated to the work of the spirit on earth. May your light shine on earth as it does in heaven.

O gracious Spirit, we thank thee for the joy and the blessing of the earth's beauty. We thank thee for life, for love, and for all the happiness which life brings to us.

In this quiet service, we lay aside all earthly thoughts and desires, and pray that we may become receptive to the outpouring of blessing of light from the world of spirit, the heavenly world, the heavenly garden. In these moments of silence we are free of all entanglements of earthly cares and demands. We pray, O gracious Spirit that we may be drawn into thy white fire. We see the multitude of shining ones, we feel their love. We are united with all forms of life for we are in thee our Creator. We are in thee, and thou art in us.

We pray that we may catch the music, the harmony of thy spirit, bringing to our souls that deep true peace of at-one-ment, at-one-ment with each other, with all those who live in the world of spirit, with all creation, at-one-ment in thee, the Great White Spirit.

*

'In the sweetness of the Lord'; we feel this sweet presence now in our midst. Pure and lovely thou art, our Father Mother. Thou art the source of our life. Thou art the beginning and the end, the complete circle, and we are within that circle. For thy all-enfolding presence, O Lord, we humbly give our thanks. Surrounding us is a great company of brethren, shining souls. We hear their music, and their prayer: 'The peace of God be with us all. Peace be unto you dear brother, sister, the peace of eternal life.'

Great White Spirit, thou who art Father Mother and Christ the Son, the light in our hearts and lives, the light which we see in manifestation in the glory of the earth, in the blessing of the sunshine, and the beauty of the awakening life in all nature; thou who dost enfold our lives and supply our every need, we thank thee for thy love. We thank thee for our creation, for the unfolding vision of the spiritual worlds, and for the demonstration of eternal life.

We open wide our hearts to the light, to the sunlight of God.

*

So let us turn our faces towards the great Sun of God, and thank God for his love; thank the Christ for the gift of eternal life, ever opening and progressing towards the finer, grander life.

A prayer for our teacher

Master and Lord, we would remember before thee our gentle Brother of the Spirit, from whom cometh neither harshness, criticism nor judgment, but only true understanding of our waywardness, true love despite all. We would pray for this gentle Brother who by sacrifice serves; and by love, unfailing love, holds before us an ideal of loving kindness.

Many has our Brother succoured, many blessed. We pray that God may crown his labours, bless his great endeavour, and prosper his harvest ... And may those who serve and labour with him give in simplicity and humility and love. We bless and thank thee, gentle Brother, in God's name.

A prayer for the Lodge*

Grant, O Loving Kindness within us all, that those who work and those who worship in the Lodge may never mistake numbers, praise, or publicity for success; may never strive for position when all service is valued and all are equal; may never seek for self; may preserve a kindly humour and go their way content to serve.

May such a spirit of fellowship abide as to silence all gossip and destructive criticism, so that all who enter find enduring peace, true kindliness, and understanding.

* Or for a church or group.

THE RADIATION OF THE STAR: PRAYERS OF CO-OPERATION

'You ask us, "White Eagle, what can we do to help mankind?" And we answer:

'There are many ways open to man. But there is one unfailing, one certain true way for man to establish God's kingdom upon earth. This is by the light which is within himself. Daily endeavour to realise your true self which is buried deep in your innermost being. Remember always the quiet, pure and true contact within the sanctuary of your own being. Be true to your own self, your own spirit, and in being true to yourself you will be true also to God and the universal brotherhood. Practise this daily realisation of the great white light within your own being and project it forth into the world of men. Then, my friends, the mists around the earth will gradually be dispelled. Do not look to others to do the work for you. Every man is his own saviour; and every man is the saviour of all mankind.

'When you come into the presence of your Creator, you come thinking thoughts of love towards your brethren, towards all life. Prayer is not only a matter of thinking about what you want—that is only a small part of the picture. The truth is that you wish to work with God to create harmony, beauty and health, holiness and happiness, not only for yourself but for all mankind. It is this motive of creative love which gives power and life to your thoughts and prayers.

'Whatever men's outward appearance, however unenlightened or different they appear to be, remember that within, deep within every soul is that spark of beauty, that seed of God which can grow. By your sincere, true thoughts of love you can project to the souls of men the light of God, and they, perhaps unconsciously, will receive that light. We in spirit look right into the heart and we know that every man and woman has within them the love of God. We know the goodness of mankind, and we advise you all to seek this goodness in your fellow man, to look for it. A master has the power to find that goodness and love in his younger brethren. He has the power to touch it and to draw it out. This is your work too, both in the outer world, and at the unseen level of life. Not to condemn or blame, even in the outer world where it is so natural for a human being to judge from surface appearances.

'When in the quietness of your sanctuary you are attuned to the Christ spirit, you are beginning to feel and know a power which is creative in life; and in your worship of God you can bring into operation the power of your higher mind to create form. Create, visualise the blazing six-pointed star, still, yet full of life and light. Identify yourselves with the star, the centre of that star; in your

47

imagination enter it, go right into the heart of that star. It is a star of the Christ love . . . so gentle, yet firm and all-powerful for good. Feel the light radiating forth to bless, to comfort, to heal . . . Hold the souls of men, or of any individual you wish to help within the heart of the star, and see them perfect in the light, the sunlight of God . . .

'When you surrender in love and simplicity to the Christ spirit, the form you are imagining is given life by the power of God. Your thought creates the form, but the love in your heart gives life to that form and sends it forth to heal the sick, to inspire peace and brotherhood in the world of men. Brothers, let us send forth the light of the Star . . .'

The star with six points is a symbol of the Christ spirit, of man made perfect. It is a symbol of the New Age. Spiritually we now stand at a new age of consciousness, when a gradual recognition will dawn that man must work in co-operation with God; that man cannot shuffle off his responsibility upon God. In this age every activity for the welfare of man will play its part, and perhaps the most potent, the most far-reaching will be that putting forth of man's own powers of the soul and spirit in the form of prayer. Men will train and dedicate themselves to this end. This will be their form of expression, their form of service to their fellows and of co-operation with higher powers.

THE WHITE EAGLE LODGE PRAYER
FOR HUMANITY

The words of the following prayer were given by White Eagle for use in the White Eagle Lodge. It can be used by all groups or individuals working simply and with dedication to radiate the light of the Christ spirit. Because of its use over many years the phrases have come to have a particular power, and with this prayer the wording should not be altered.

Prayer

Let us remember before God the great need of mankind; and that we may pray to God, let us make quiet the fretful daily mind ... Let us open our hearts to the Father Mother God, and to Christ the Son—to the holy Trinity of wisdom ... love ... and power.

In the holy name of Christ, by the Christ light in the hearts of men, we call upon the great angels of Christ; we feel their presence and their power . . . we attune ourselves to the prayers of all men of goodwill . . .

Being thus prepared and ready before God . . . with all the will of our minds, with all the love of our deepest heart, *we send forth the light* . . .

We send it forth as a great star of light . . . a star of light . . . a blazing star . . . withstanding, overcoming all evil, triumphant over death . . . a star of the Christ light.

By all the power of Christ within, we send forth the light . . .

*

Let us now hold within this great healing star any soul known to us personally who is in need of this help. Silently we name them★ and see them perfect in the heart of the star.

★ *The names can be called aloud when this is appropriate.*

If you work on your own rather than in a group, and have a busy active life, you may prefer to use this shortened version. Many people in different countries of the world use one of these two prayers, particularly at 12.00 noon each day—and if they cannot manage this time, at any of the hours of 3, 6, and 9: these hours have their own particularly helpful 'vibration'. The length of time spent is not important, but if you can leave for a brief time all your immediate preoccupations and concentrate on the blazing star for a few moments, you will have made a contribution. The strength of your work will come through making the effort regularly each day. As you do this you may begin to feel that you are not working alone, but as one of a brotherhood, all working to make their contribution to the healing of individuals and nations.

DAILY HEALING PRAYER

Say in your heart:

We hold all humanity in the golden light of the Christ star and see the power of the Son of God working in the hearts of men . . .

We behold the blazing star, with the form of the Lord Christ within its centre, radiating God's healing power and spirit of love to all mankind . . . We hold all who have asked for help or healing within this golden healing light . . .

May God's blessing be on this work.

Here also is a healing prayer, a prayer of co-operation. It falls into three parts: first, attunement to God and God's angels; second, attunement to the patient; third, the projection of power by a group (or by one person—with the substitution of 'I' and 'me' for 'we' and 'us'). A unified and harmonious group is always the more powerful.

We bow mind and heart in prayer before God ... We silence the outer self and banish worldly matters and thoughts. With deep and compassionate love for all mankind we await the incoming of the Spirit ... Spiritual power now encompasses us. Steadily, quietly, deeply, we breathe in the Spirit of God ... We pray: Fill us, O Spirit—fill us—fill us—and bless our endeavour to heal.

Being thus attuned, and steadfast in the light of God and the power of God's angels, we remember all those who are sick and who suffer . . . We especially concentrate upon ——

Here three times speak the full name of each patient

We hold him (or her) in a ray of spiritual light. We concentrate and project healing power to ——

Here again speak the sufferer's full name

We behold him (or her) as helped, as healed, as made perfect in God . . .

Create this vision of the patient whole and perfect in the light

We thank thee Lord for thy presence, and the blessing of thy healing grace on these thy children.

It is important that each word should be given its full value, and that there be a pause between each sentence; for power is gathered during silence, whereas hasty, careless speech can disperse power. The three parts of the service should be carefully studied; first, the attunement to God; second, the linking with the patient; third, the sending forth of healing power to the patient. For each part has its definite purpose, combining to make a short but complete service.

Strength, encouragement or support can be sent to any man or woman, or to a group working for some ideal in social or national life. The wording or form of service can be correspondingly amended. The essence of the matter is simply that this is *active* prayer, whereas much prayer lacks this quality of purposefulness.

White Eagle says: 'The early Christian Brotherhood learnt that by developing the inner light in themselves, by their life, their thought, their ready service, their attitude towards their fellow creatures—by developing warm love and sympathy, by manifesting joy and happiness within themselves, which reached out to touch the soul of others, they were able to give consolation and healing to all who suffered. This grace of which we speak is the power to console the dying, to console those who mourn.

'When you become stronger in the light of the Star you will find that ill-health, pain and sorrow will recede. But this cannot happen to the man who lives entirely for material thoughts and objects. It comes to the meek, the simple and the lowly who are, in their souls, brothers of that inner light.

'Each individual soul can make an effort to start to understand what is meant by this inner light. Every soul can give itself in service to humanity. Service on the outer plane is of value. Service on the inner planes, in the silence, is of greater value still. Even in your loneliness you can work to send out this beautiful and true light, the Christ light, which is love. But you must direct it with purpose and with knowledge. Ordinary prayer is just an asking for something for self, or for someone else. What the Brotherhood is endeavouring to teach mankind, is a positive, constructive, unshakeable thought of God . . . God in everything, God everywhere—God who has power to restore, to heal and to comfort man.'

THE POWER OF AFFIRMATION

Many people have had the experience at some time in their lives of feeling themselves as part of an infinite spirit, if only for a fleeting moment; they have felt themselves to be one with something far larger and more all-embracing than their human personality. If this is in a way a humbling experience it has still left an awareness that there is that within their hearts that beats in tune with a great spirit of love.

The effort that a man makes to lay aside the material thoughts that bind and limit him and to aspire with his mind on God, is often an effort to find the strength and the love to meet the opportunities and responsibilities life brings to him; but it is this effort too that helps him perhaps unconsciously to grow a little more at one with the Father Mother God.

As he becomes stronger, he begins to find he can draw on the power of God within him to control his life—to bring harmony to his being. He affirms the God within him, affirms that there is a spark of the divine within his heart centre. It is through this Christ spirit that he eventually becomes consciously at one with God; and it is also through this Christ spirit that he can establish health in his own 'kingdom' of body, mind and soul.

This chapter is based on White Eagle's teaching on the power of affirmation, of how to affirm the Christ-like qualities within the soul. The main theme of the chapter is how to put into practice the maxim 'heal thyself'. We thought it might be helpful to open the chapter with a picture White Eagle once gave of Red Indian life; it seems such a beautiful evocation of a people who knew how to draw on the power of God in human life, and knew too how to live in harmony with all nature.

This passage is taken from Grace Cooke's book
THE ILLUMINED ONES:

'We come back from the spirit-life to bring
a little knowledge and urge you to listen, try
out our suggestions about right thought.
Right thought is God thought, good thought,
goodwill, which brings right action. It brings
control of the nervous system, correct breathing, quiet, steady living. Can you see an old
Indian chief getting in a panic and rushing
about? Try to imagine him in all his regalia,
entering the circle of his people in silence,
quietly perambulating, sprinkling incense,
giving his blessing. See him standing with
arms upraised invoking the love and blessing
of his Creator. Can you hear the steady beat of
those countless Indians who will follow him at
a given moment, in procession, chanting?
What are they chanting? Can you not imagine
it? They are chanting in harmony with life's
rhythm, chanting the great AUM, invoking
the power of the spirit, creating, drawing

even on the wind currents to bring something wholly good, a physical and spiritual blessing on the community of tribes.'

Whenever man seeks spiritual truth and understanding he must look upward, must rise in spirit, in consciousness leaving behind the earth, and earthly planes. The imprisoned splendour which is within the soul of man must be released. It has to be resurrected, it must arise. When Jesus said 'I am the resurrection and the life', he meant that the I AM, or the Christ Spirit in the heart of man, is the resurrection and is the life. 'I AM the way, the truth and the life.' The I AM is not the little earth self. The I AM is the part of God within the heart of every man. The I AM is the Christ, the sun, the light within the human heart.

The affirmations which follow call upon this inner self, the Christ self to rise and take control of the life and rule the kingdom of the self.

In using them, first try to visualise the form and gentle presence of the Lord Christ beside you and know that as well as being apart from you, his spirit also dwells within you. Try to imagine what the Master would say or do in the circumstances in which you find yourself.

Seek to identify yourself with the Master, to feel as he would feel, to love as he would love; feel from him his divine love enveloping you, penetrating your heart and bringing to life the emotion of divine love in yourself; and then affirm:

I AM DIVINE LOVE

Say the words from the God within your heart, the I AM within which is all love . . . Say them over again, several times. Dwell on the thought of the love of God in you which can transcend your human frailty, and which is the gentle master of your life.

*

Be still, and look into the shining Christ

star. From the centre of this star, the light and the strength and the wisdom of God your heavenly Father flows into your heart and your whole being is filled with light. Say:

I AM IN THE LIGHT . . . I GIVE LIGHT . . . AND I BLESS AND RAISE ALL MEN UP INTO THE LIGHT.

*

Are you ruffled, upset, disappointed, annoyed? Think then of the Master, feel his gentle presence and say, deep within yourself, peace . . . peace . . . peace to the waves of emotion, the waves of fear, the waves of doubt. Peace . . .

Affirm:

I AM DIVINE PEACE

Say the words many times over. Think of a still and shining sea; of how the Master stilled the winds and storm. Or consider the beautiful word tranquil—the tranquil mind, the tranquil heart, the tranquil life. Here in this word is your ideal—dwell upon it.

*

You are confused, cannot decide what to do about a particular problem? Or you long for wisdom? Know that the Christ dwelling within you is all wise. Let this Christ within arise and affirm:

I AM DIVINE WISDOM

Say it deeply, powerfully, many times. Then wait to be shown. Have courage to wait upon God. Divine wisdom will point the way.

If you can keep your certain sure contact with God, nothing can go wrong in your life. You will then have no need to worry about decisions for they will be made for you. But you must be quickened in spirit, so that you will respond instantly to the gentle guidance of the almighty Presence within you.

*

You are tired, a little battered by life? You feel you really cannot face up to things, cannot carry on? Do not permit yourself to be dragged down by doubts and fears. The power of Christ within is strong, it is mighty, it can accomplish all things, for it is of God. Say from your heart:

I AM DIVINE POWER

Say it until courage returns. Keep on saying it. The power of the spirit of Christ within you will enable you to rise and carry your burden as though it did not exist. Christ in you will rise triumphant over earth.

*

When you are in the shadows or feel that the shadows are near, look up, visualise the blazing Sun above you in the spirit spheres, feel its strength, its steadiness pouring into your heart. Say:

I AM IN THE SUN . . . THE SUN OF
GOD IS IN ME

Feel that you are in the Sun, part of the Sun, filled with the strength of the Sun in your heart. Then go forward in the full consciousness of the light of the Sun shining upon you and in you.

*

You are depressed and fearful? There is no strength, no health in you? Refuse the conflict of earthly thought; refuse to be held down by depressing darkness of a material world. Remember the power of God in you to make all things new.

Affirm:

I AM PERFECT AS MY FATHER CREATED
ME PERFECT

Say it many times, until the realisation becomes part of you. You, the child of God are whole, you are holy, and as you truly and earnestly think, so you become.

*

If you find it difficult to control your emotions, or when the choice before you seems too hard, at those moments breathe quietly and deeply and say to yourself many times:

GOD IS WITHIN ME

Then be still, and let all-good manifest through you.

*

Finally, because we ourselves have found it so helpful, and to end on a note of joy, we are quoting from the book MEDITATION.

'Breathe calmly and rhythmically, slowly visualising within yourself the dawning spiritual light, and in it, the form of the Lord Christ. As you absorb this light and this gentle, loving nature—that is, feeling that your true nature is his nature, worshipping and adoring his perfection of life—you can then feel welling up within you the intense joy of the spirit.

This gift for feeling joy is part of our Christnature. In our meditation, we see ourselves and our world in a light which floods our being with joy.

We find within us a Presence which opens the way into worlds invisible and glorious.

We are bathed in joy, we touch the loftiest height of human and spiritual joy. Our being sings with joy, dances with joy.

We find that life itself is joy, and we are reborn into a tangible world of joy. As the Psalmist sings, "In thy presence is fulness of joy".'

White Eagle has further said:

The bread, the 'I AM' is the Supreme One, is God-consciousness, and the heart of man is the holy grail filled by the divine essence of pure love. When man can partake of the sustaining bread, the life-giving wine, when he can take holy communion with the one Supreme, he will know eternal life. The law of love brings into being the galaxies of stars, it creates all nature; it causes the spider to spin, and the bee to gather honey, the bird to sing, and the rose to give forth its fragrance. It is the one supreme law operating through every kingdom of nature, through every plane of physical life, through the astral and mental, the celestial and the heavenly planes to which man will eventually pass. Those who have taken true communion, who have eaten the bread of life become free on these planes of heavenly consciousness even while in the physical body. The 'I AM' is no longer an obscurity. The 'I AM' in them reaches out to enfold all creation, reaches up to be absorbed into the very heart of God.

PRAYERS OF ASPIRATION

This chapter opens with a passage of White Eagle's teaching where he talks of breathing in the breath of God, and the help that the correct practice of breathing is in putting oneself in tune with life, with God. All the prayers in this section were spoken in a voice that seemed to carry the stillness and the firmness of deep breathing; but also a completely natural, loving voice, without any strain.

Some of these 'prayers of aspiration' are simple thoughts to the Creator, others are deeper mystical prayers. Saying a prayer aloud does have its own power, as White Eagle says elsewhere in this book; but we hope also that people will find that silent reading helps them to make their own spoken or unspoken prayer within, and to feel themselves in touch with an infinite, loving spirit, even when most in the middle of life; and also when sitting in an 'upper room' for spiritual work. These prayers of aspiration do not ask for spiritual gain or material benefit, they just voice the soul's aspiration to draw closer to the heart of love and to express the light, the love, the will of God in human life. They should too bring healing and strength in times of suffering and difficulty, and added happiness in times of joy. They all in different ways say 'Thy will be done on earth as it is in heaven'.

The passages of teaching beginning each group of prayers are just extracts from White Eagle's talks which we hope will make clear the spirit of the prayers themselves.

We often speak to you of breathing in the holy breath. What is the holy breath? It is harmony. When you try to breathe in the breath of God you are breathing in harmony, healing. There is much to learn about the art of breathing, for the way you perform this simple act can affect your whole life—your spiritual unfoldment and your physical, mental and spiritual health. At this moment, relax your mind and body, and breathe deeply, quietly and slowly. As you breathe in, try to imagine that you are breathing in light and life; that you are not only inhaling air, you are filling every particle of your being with God's breath. As you do this you will naturally be freed from the problems that constrict you, because your whole mind will be on God. You will always find relief from the bondage of cares and limitations if you will practise this deep 'God-breathing'; it will bring you a sense of peace, poise and control.

As you breathe, slowly, rhythmically, calmly, at the same time forgetting the earth, raise your thoughts, your aspiration to the world above, the world of spirit. Breathe in the fragrance of the rose. Breathe in the light of God. Breathe out the love of God. Be still and know God. Peace . . . peace . . . be still.

THE WHITE EAGLE LODGE PRAYER
OF DEDICATION

May the light of Christ shining in my heart stand guard over my thoughts and guide my speech and actions into ways of service.

May the light of Christ shine from my heart
> To heal the sick in mind and body;
> To comfort the bereaved;
> To sustain the weary.

May the light of Christ illumine my understanding and the understanding of all men, bringing true vision and awareness of the eternal life, and of the Christ within all mankind.

'When you enter this Lodge,★ remember "I enter this Lodge in the spirit of service". You enter to worship, to forget for a brief space the physical life, and feel your oneness with God; and to give service. You have come to serve, we in spirit have also come to serve. We need your service; you need the ministration of the spirit beings and friends. And so we mingle to serve each other, and to serve all men on their path to the Father Mother God.

'Remember again, that there are hosts of healing angels here, and they are directing their healing rays upon you. They can heal your body; they can heal your soul. But in order to receive this healing power, it is necessary for you to have the will and readiness

★ *These words of White Eagle were addressed to members of the White Eagle Lodge but can be applied to any group.*

78

to love and serve others; as you give, so you shall receive. If you can, take this keynote out into your life tomorrow—the tomorrow which begins the life of the everyday, the life of workshop and factory, warehouses and offices and schools, and the many varying phases of activity. Take into this world the will to serve. You do not work because you can get something by so doing; you work to serve. Many whom you contact you will feel do not deserve your service and love. But remember, they may be suffering, they may have sorrows of which you know not; their souls may be troubled. Bear then, sympathy towards them. Many, as you travel the road of life, need your help; and your work, if you are to fulfil your creation, is to serve them with wisdom and love. It is this service which brings dignity and humility to the heart of man.'

*

To give healing

Great White Spirit of the open sky, the mountain heights, the defiles and winding valleys; great Spirit of Love, who hast given abundance to thy children, teach us to receive thy healing power, the bread of thy spirit. May eternal wisdom nourish each waiting heart; may we thy children be caught up in the power of spiritual vision and so learn to distinguish the real from the unreal. May each soul be strengthened . . .

Thus may we lay upon the altar of thy service . . . ourselves.

The simple home of love

Great Spirit of love, we only pray to become more aware of your glory; that our light may grow more bright, more steady, so that others travelling along life's journey may see the light, and be welcomed to the simple home of

love which we would build for all the way-
farers on the path of life.

A brotherhood prayer

Great Architect of the Universe, we assemble
again with one accord to receive from thy
ministers divine truth of life and being. We,
thy servants, being duly prepared, present
ourselves before thee, awaiting thy commands.
With thy wisdom in our hearts, thy beauty in
our vision, and thy will in our minds may we
go forward to complete thy work in thy Name,
to thine honour and glory. So mote it be!

Grace

All that brings joy and light to human
hearts is the Master's work. May God's blessing be on our activity, our enjoyment, our
service.

Servers of mankind

O Great Spirit, Father Mother God . . . unto
thee be all praise, honour, glory and thanksgiving now and for ever and ever. Thou only
art real, thou only art light, thou alone art
peace, thou art all love.

Love . . . divine love quicken our hearts that
we may be servers of mankind, loving, serene,
certain of our path.

So may we enter into the great peace, the
eternal peace, the eternal love, the only reality,
the only true life.

May the light shine

Divine Spirit, we are thankful to thee for all
that is beautiful and progressive and lovely in
our life. May we never forget thy love, nor
our brother's need for thy love. We pray to
become more worthy channels through which
thy light may shine in the darkened places of
life.

'Beloved friends, when we sit in the silence and commune with the invisible, we become aware of the praise and thanksgiving flowing from the heart of God. It may seem strange to you to think of God giving thanks, but we ask you to consider this idea of God pouring forth thankfulness. God created the world, the heavens and all things. And God gave thanks when he beheld his creation. We want to put into your heart this thought of a continual outpouring of thanksgiving for everything— for life, for food, for the joy of living, even for those experiences which may appear to be bitter, for even these hold blessing for the child of God. We ponder on this idea of giving thanks for all that we have received, all that we have been able to give; we give thanks to God, to life, to the universe. As soon as we enter into the innermost sanctuary to worship

God in spirit and in truth, we must always feel the opening of the gates of praise and thanksgiving. If a soul has reached that point on his spiritual journey when he can rise from earth into heaven and dwell there for a time, one of the grand themes of which he is conscious is that of praise and thanksgiving. And we too, on earth, can join in this grand symphony.

'We have to reach beyond the visible to the invisible. Many souls are continually thanking God who do not appear to be very religious. They seem to be very ordinary people, but when we look more closely we notice that they are enjoying life, that they have the ability always to touch something in life which is beautiful. They enjoy the food which comes to them from God's bounty. They listen to music and are raised into an ecstasy of thanksgiving; they behold the flowers and see not merely the flower, but also God in that flower. They may not label him by name, they may not say that God is speaking through the flower, but their souls gaze upon the woodlands and the bright flowers and from them receive happiness; they are forever touching the invisible and intangible, although they may not call it God.

'Such souls may not sing hymns or fall on their knees in prayer but theirs is an ever-present worship, they live in the presence of God. Thankfulness is one form of prayer. And, brethren, close to thanksgiving is acceptance. Acceptance comes from within, a quiet inner knowing that what comes to us today is the fruit of what we have sown with our own hands; seeds which we have planted either in this present life, or perhaps centuries ago. But whatever comes today is the harvest of our own sowing, therefore we accept this harvest with humility and thankfulness, knowing that it comes to teach and to help us become simple and to know the Creator in a way that we would not otherwise have attained . . .'

A moment's thought

Thou who art our Father God, the Great White Spirit of the open prairie and wind-swept sky, the flowers and the rain, and the quiet running waters; thou who dost speak to us from the hearts of those we love; unto thee we come, full of thankfulness for the joy of life. May each one respond to thy blessing of love, and may this peace enfold all those who walk the path of life.

The prayer of a child-like heart

Our loving Father and Mother, we thank you for all beauty; for the love of friends, for the kindness we meet each day, for the joy of serving others—for all this gracious world. We thank you for any act of ours which has brought happiness to others. We thank you for one another, for all you have given to us—for peaceful sleep and the hour of waking; and for the bread of earth and heaven which sustains our body and our soul.

For the companionship and affection of animals we thank you; for all people who labour for our sustenance; and for the law, order, and harmony which can control our inner life.

We pray, O God, that we may so live as to draw closer to understanding, and to the deep peace of the universal heart; to that peace which is indeed of you, beloved, beloved our Father—our Mother, all-good ... God!

PEACE

'With a serene and tranquil mind and heart' ... this is one of the most difficult conditions to which man, placed in the vortex of human life, can attain; but we would emphasise the great need there is for all souls who aspire to the White Lodge above, to learn the secret and the power of a tranquil and serene mind. We advise you, beloved children, to pray amid the turmoil of your earthly life, for calmness of mind and heart. May this be your daily prayer; and when you have attained to a degree of calmness, you will not find it difficult to love. You must earnestly pray to unfold these two qualities.

Without there is the bustle, turmoil and noise of the outer plane, so typical of man's life on earth. But within this Lodge there is peace, there is love.

This is a very good example to you of the lodge which is within your heart, the true temple of the spirit. In your outer life, in the outer courts, there is inharmony, harshness, noise and disturbing elements. In the heart there may always be peace, stillness and love.

The Master's voice is the Christ within your heart. O beloved brethren, we understand your individual difficulties, we know how hard it is for you to prevent the impatient 'mob' from invading your inner lodge. But this you have to learn to do. This is your work as a brother. You have to retain the peace and sanctity of the lodge within, and so control the outer court that you can hear the voice of the Master . . .

If you could see with pure spiritual vision, you would see into the hearts of all men and you would find beneath all the rubble and the rubbish a great sweetness. Try to cultivate true vision, so that you may see the sweetness in your brother's heart. At the present time it is only God or one of the wise ones who can see that sweetness in every human heart, but you are all being trained to do just this: to look into the darkness and see the shining light.

A moment of quietness

O Divine Presence, we breathe in the breath of stillness, we open our hearts to thee. Thou knowest the need of thy children. We do not ask, we aspire to become more in tune with thy love. So shall the peace of thy spirit dwell within us, and we shall know that all is well.

A Red Indian prayer

Deep peace of the open prairie and the wind-swept sky, the flowing rivers, the quiet valleys and the noble trees standing stalwart and true on the mountain side, steady through all the boisterous winds of life ... deep peace of God dwell within us, giving us a like strength, to bring us back to thee, our Father.

Thy hand in mine

Father, give unto me thy Spirit that I may overcome the world which is so much with me, which troubles body and mind. May thy love so sustain me that I may be strong in thee, walking with thy hand in mine, my heart beating with thine, and my life held safe in thee.

To live in harmony

Eternal Spirit, Father Mother God, I seek thy Presence.

I close the door of my outer senses to enter into thy temple, the temple of my heart, and in the stillness of the spirit I worship thee, Creator Lord.

I aspire in thankfulness; praying for understanding of life's experience, and of the laws of the spiritual universe.

My mind is open to truth . . .

My heart is full of love towards every creature.

May thy spirit lead me to the centre of harmony, to the life of harmony, in which is perfect health and holiness.

White Eagle was talking after a reading of St Matthew Chapter 5:

'In the gospel stories of Jesus it says "Seeing the multitude, he went up into a high mountain, and when he was set, his disciples came to him". Now according to the earthly interpretation, the mountain was a real one, outside the city of Jerusalem. This may have been so, but we say also that it was a mountain of consciousness, that Jesus raised himself above the earthly consciousness. Jesus, the pure, clear recipient of the light and the wisdom of God, had to be raised in consciousness before he descended to the plains, or onto the physical level of life, to teach the multitude. The disciples, those who would follow the Master, came unto him; they too raised their consciousness. They did not expect to understand the word of God and the inner mysteries, unless they raised their consciousness onto a higher plane. Man cannot wholly comprehend spiritual truth with his mind or at the material level. The intellect is very necessary and must be developed before the soul can comprehend the grandeur of the cosmos; nevertheless, the intellect can make the spirit of man its prisoner and bind it, so that the divine intelligence in man is unable to function. This is the mistake and danger of the over-development of the intellect of man today. But when that intellect is guided and led by the light within, so that the intellect becomes the instrument for the divine intelligence, for the knowledge and wisdom which comes from the heaven world, then the intellect is taking its correct place in the evolution of man and in the development of man's life here on earth.

Thus we say that there are two aspects of life —the outer and the inner. Man tries to understand God with his intellect, and he reads books and others' opinions, he analyses and criticises and thinks he has arrived at truth.

But that is not the way, my friends; the way to truth is the way of the spirit, is the way of the light from within man's heart. It is to understand and unfold all those spiritual faculties with which God has endowed his son/daughter on this earth plane. It is by way of meditation and contemplation, as the saints taught. But even this is not enough. Man may meditate all his life on the glories of the heaven world and still be unable to reach his goal. God intended man on earth to be perfectly balanced between spirit and matter, between the divine life and the material life. Hence the symbol of the star, representing the perfectly balanced man, and representing too the Christ spirit which must find expression in daily life, in gentleness, in humility, kindness and courtesy, in accepting God as the one true source of life. Side by side with your communion, it is in your effort to serve and from your human experience that you will gain entry into the mysteries of life.

An open mind

O Great Spirit of life and truth, we pray that our consciousness may be ever enlarged and widened, that we may comprehend love and brotherhood in life. We thank thee for this blessing of brotherhood and communion with spirit ... Here, in the stillness, we make the pledge to be strong to accept the experience which comes to us, knowing that it comes as an opportunity to expand and purify our vision. May we be true to our higher self, which has asked for light.

Before listening to teaching

My brethren, let us with one accord approach the heart of all wisdom and love; let us close the outer courts and enter the sanctuary of silence, praying with bowed heads, bowed intellects ... Father Mother, blessed God, we come to commune with thee to absorb thy rays of light and life; we thank thee for thy Son, the light within our breast. May this light shine forth in our lives both here and in the spheres beyond, so that we may live to add to thy glory, for ever and ever.

'Whenever you find yourselves becoming over-anxious, excited, overwrought about daily happenings, either in the outer world or in your personal life, pause and remember, "The Lord is my shepherd, I shall not want".

' "The Lord is my shepherd." What does this mean? Simply, it means that God has created you his child in his own image and has breathed into you the breath of his life. This does not mean only the physical breath and the life of the physical body, it means that you are a part of God; God has breathed into your whole being his divine love, his divine life. In your inmost being you are part of him—one with God, with the divine intelligence which watches over every detail of your human life.

'This is difficult for you to understand with your finite mind. You cannot conceive of an intelligence able to enter into your every thought and feeling, to guide wisely every event of your life; and to take you, when you die, gently, beautifully and peacefully through the gateway into that heaven world from which you came. A long time has passed, my children, since you left that heavenly home, that world of sunlight, the spiritual sun from which you all originated; and so you forget that you are spirit, born of God, and eternally linked with him. You have to learn consciously to remember that you are a part of this eternal spiritual sun. Seek the light, my children; rise from the earth and turn your faces to the sun, breathing in the breath of life from your Father who is in heaven, who gathers to himself in due time every one of his children, all the world over and throughout all time.

'Daily seek the presence of God. Remember every morning as you wake and every evening as you go to rest that you are held within the love of your heavenly Father Mother, and you will be uplifted and relieved of all tension. Open your heart to the inflow of that great Sun-life, till your whole being, body and soul and spirit, becomes charged again and again with divine Life flowing eternally from the heart of God.'

Before going to sleep

Great White Spirit, Father of love and peace, fold us to thy heart that we may rest upon thy breast, and receive from thee that strength of spirit and illumination which will cause us to awaken with joy and with a desire to live to bring truth and joy upon earth. Father, we thank thee.

Surrender all

We open our hearts to the Great White Spirit . . .

Thou who art Father Mother God, whose Son is the Christ of all humanity, we worship thee; we thank thee for our creation and all the blessings of life. Even when we are called to walk in the shadow-land, we know that thou art with us; that thou art bringing us through darkness into the glory of thy life. We surrender all to thy love. Knowing that thou art love we have no fear.

Security

We would leave you with a sense of deep security and peace. Focus your thoughts upon God, all-good ... place your trust in God. Let nothing disturb you. Put your hand in the hand of the Divine Son, even Christ. No harm can touch you, nothing hurt you. This is eternal truth.

Into thy loving heart we come, O Lord; we are enfolded within thy pure aura of love.

Unto thee we surrender all that we have and

are. All happiness and joy are thine, and come from thee. Unto thee be thanksgiving, for ever and for ever.

'The Master enfolds you in his love, knowing your heart and your need. But he knows also that the problems and difficulties of your earthly life are part of your karma, and he helps you by helping you to command yourself.

'It is not what is happening around you that is important. It is the way you deal with such happenings.

'You can get worked up and make yourselves ill, as some of you have done, and may do again; or you can keep very still, and continually seek the place of silence and strength. Having stilled the emotions, the next step is to reach the innermost centre of communion and the intaking of strength. You can then examine your problem and say, "Dear God,

* *This passage is from the White Eagle book*
  HEAL THYSELF

I would have the strength to handle this as the Master would handle it".

'In the presence of the Master anger and resentment dissolve. You are raised above the pulls and antagonisms of the earthly plane. You are filled with peace, overcome with adoration and love.

'If you are big and wise enough to do what we say, you will never again be torn by emotion, nor will you be puzzled; because there, within yourself, you will find the still, ever-burning flame, so bright, a flame of the spiritual sun. As you concentrate on that pure, bright, white flame, you will feel the majesty of the sun in yourself: you will know you are master of your body and the conditions of your life. Nothing can touch you. That Presence deep, deep within you is the I AM. "Be still and know that I AM God."

'When you can make that contact, my children, all your worries will fall into place; the pattern will become perfect.'

Have the courage to live by the knowledge and the wisdom which comes to you in these silent moments of prayer and aspiration; see the right way and follow it in spite of darkness and ignorance. By thinking rightly, by speaking rightly, and by feeling love and brotherhood to all creatures, you are helping to awaken the light in the heart of your brother and helping him to understand the true meaning of life and of God's love.

INDEX OF PRAYERS BY TITLE